SANTA ANNA

PATRIOT OR SCOUNDREL

SANTA ANNA
PATRIOT OR SCOUNDREL

RUBY C. TOLLIVER

Hendrick-Long Publishing Co.
P.O. BOX 25123 • DALLAS, TEXAS 75225

LIBRARY OF CONGRESS CATALOGING-IN-PUBLICATION DATA

Tolliver, Ruby C.
    Santa Anna: patriot or scoundrel / Ruby C. Tolliver
        p.   cm.
    Includes bibliographical references and index.
    Summary: Describes the life of the soldier and politician who was president
of Mexico eleven times and defeated Texan troops at the Battle of the Alamo.
    ISBN 0-937460-82-6
    1. Santa Anna, Antonio López de. 1794?-1876 — Juvenile literature.
2. Mexico—History—1821-1861—Juvenile literature.   3. Texas—History—
To 1846 — Juvenile literature.   4. Presidents — Mexico — Biography —
Juvenile literature.   5. Generals — Mexico — Biography — Juvenile
literature. [1. Santa Anna, Antonio López de, 1794?-1876.   2. Presidents —
Mexico.   3. Mexico — History — 1821-1861.]
I. Title.
F1232.S232T65   1992
972'.04'092—dc20   92-33092
[B]   CIP
                                                                                            AC

Design and production: Shadow Canyon Graphics, Evergreen, Colorado
Map: Michael Taylor, Prescott, Arizona

ILLUSTRATIONS:

Courtesy Special Collections Division, The University of Texas at Arlington Libraries, Arlington, Texas: pages iii, 63, 73, 80, and 83

Courtesy The Center for American History, The University of Texas at
Austin: pages 35, 46, 49, and 87

Courtesy The General Libraries of The University of Texas at Austin,
Benson Latin American Collection: page 74

Courtesy Hendrick-Long Collection: pages 21 and 31

Printed in the United States of America

Hendrick-Long Publishing Company
Dallas, Texas 75225-1123

Table of Contents

To
Halon and Herman Landry,
special friends

Preface

Students of Mexican history know who Santa Anna was. Students of Texas history know who Santa Anna was. Students of most of the western states' histories should also know who Santa Anna was.

Santa Anna wished to be known as:

El Presidente
Napoleon of the West
Benemérito de la Patria
The Liberator
Perpetual Dictator
His Serene Highness
A Good Mexican
Well-Deserving of the Fatherland

After doing much research, I could only call him:

Patriot or Scoundrel

— *Ruby C. Tolliver*
1992

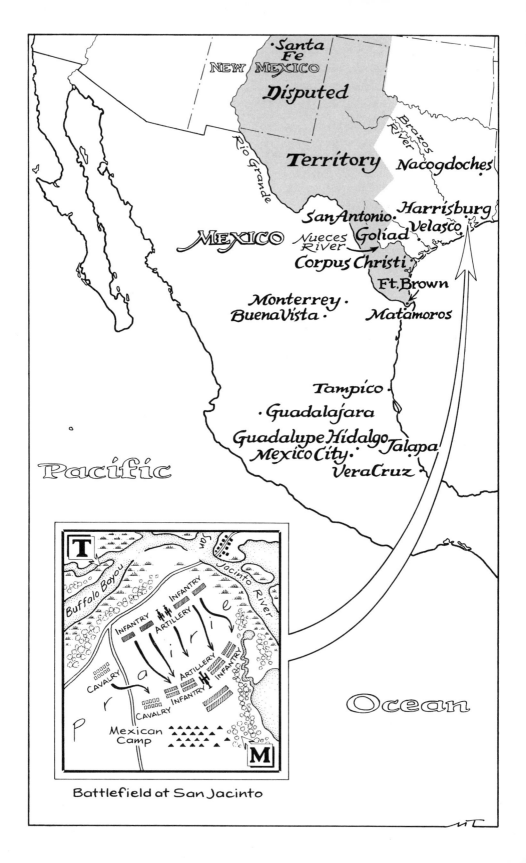

Battlefield at San Jacinto

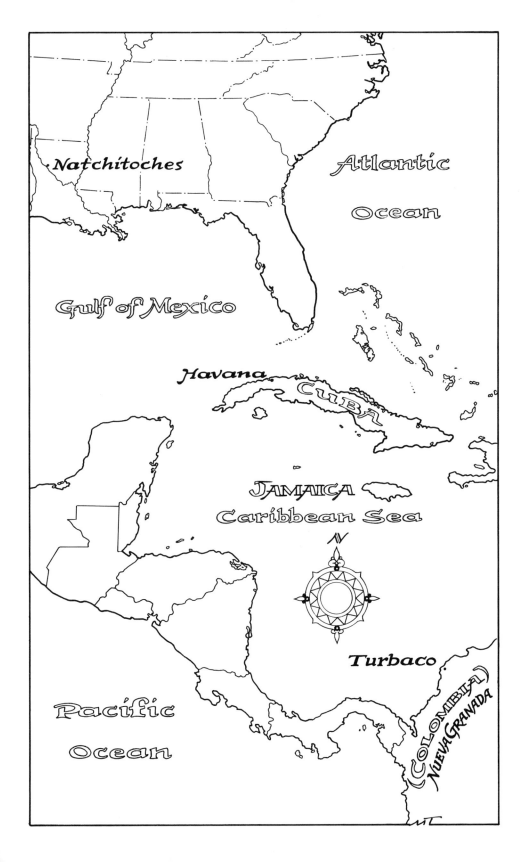

El Presidente: An Introduction

Mexico is an interesting country whose destiny is yet shrouded in doubt. Once our sovereign, all its early annals are part of our past.

For two hundred years, Spanish governors and commandants were the rulers of Texas and the other Spanish-American States; and portraits of Bustamente and Santa Anna might hang in the gallery of governors of seven of our states.

When Santa Anna made his mad march across Texas in 1836, he held the future of all the Southwest in his hands.

With six companies of grenadiers, he reached Morgan's Point on April 20th, and sat on his horse where the tide comes in at Bay Ridge, and looked out upon the Mexican Sea which washed the shores of his vast empire — a country which reached from Yucatan to Oregon, and whose area was greater than any other nation of the world, save Russia.

And when he turned back from the bay that day, he went to San Jacinto, to fight the sixteenth decisive battle in the history of the world.

This generation may well be interested in these stirring events, and in the career of one of our former rulers, who fought more battles than Washington and Napoleon combined.

C. R. Wharton
Houston, October 5, 1924

El Presidente: A SKETCH OF THE LIFE OF GENERAL SANTA ANNA,
Clarence R. Wharton

In the Beginning

"No! Antonio! It is my turn to be general." Ten-year-old Manuel knocked the wooden sword from Antonio's hand. Antonio did not strike back. Even though they were the same age, Antonio knew Manuel was stronger. Antonio knew he must outwit Manuel in order to remain the general, the leader. His brown eyes sparkled as he planned.

"All right, Manuel, you can be the general now." Antonio picked up his sword from the dusty road and moved to the back of the line. "Go ahead, General Manuel. It is time for you to take the troops across the river to safety." Antonio waved his hand motioning "the troops," five young *mestizo* boys (Indian/Spanish) to follow Manuel.

"Do we have to cross the river?" Manuel asked.

"Yes, of course." Antonio knew Manuel was afraid of the river. Antonio was, too, but Manuel did not know that.

"Then you can be the general, Antonio. I should stay on this side and watch for Indians. We forgot about them."

A sly smile tugged at Antonio's lips. They had not forgotten. It was Manuel's excuse for not wanting to cross the river. Now, as general, Antonio knew he must think of something so he would not have to cross the river with the troops. He bowed his head like he had seen the *alcalde* (town mayor) do before answering the complaints of the citizens here in Jalapa, Vera Cruz, Mexico.

"Antonio?" Manuel was growing impatient.

Throwing back his skinny shoulders, Antonio ordered, "I have decided. We should not cross the river." Before Manuel or the others could protest, he explained. "The Indians would chase us across the river. They are riding ponies and would knock us down. We would all drown," he added, his voice low and solemn. Antonio had watched the traveling troupes of actors perform each time they came to Jalapa. He knew, even at the age of ten, how to convince his audience.

"Manuel," he ordered, "you are the best shooter. You must keep the Indians from turning past the house of Belen. I and the others will wait in ambush at the river."

Not waiting for his playmates to protest or agree, Antonio ran to crouch behind a nearby stand of oleanders. Using his sword, he pointed to the other trees as he cried, "Hide there, Adan, you and Pedro, behind the poinsettias." He waved his sword at the smallest soldiers. "Iggie, Jaime, Cero, hurry or you will be scalped. Get behind the woodpile." The boys hurried to obey his commands, their stick muskets on their shoulders.

Antonio and his friends played soldiers with their imaginary Indian foes until they were called home for their evening meals. That night as the stars came out and the moon began to rise, Antonio Lopez de Santa Anna Perez de Lebron settled down to sleep and to dream of the day he would be a real general in the army of New Spain (Mexico).

Four years later, in 1808, Antonio stood before his father and pleaded, "Please, Papa. Do not apprentice me to Señor Martinez. I do not want to be a tile merchant. I do not want to be a storekeeper. I want to join the army."

"No, my son. The army is filled with men who destroy, steal and kill. Sometimes it is without cause. Yet," he slowly shook his head in puzzled fashion, "I know they have needs. Even the good soldiers often do not know when their next meal will be."

"Papa, do not blame them for taking food and clothes. We owe them that for protecting us."

"Protecting us from whom? We are a divided country. Every time the wind changes we must switch loyalties." He spit on the ground to show his disgust. "Who will be the next *caudillo* (military chieftain) to claim us for himself or a rich landowner?"

"Whoever he is will get my loyalty," boasted Antonio.

"That is if you are not shot before you turn traitor to

our present leader and his soldiers!"

"I will not be shot! I am too cunning for that. I am not stupid like most." His sneering remark and the look on his face seemed to include his father.

His father grabbed him by the shirt front and shook him. "If you ever speak to me with that tone of voice, I will not shoot you, but I will get my whip."

Antonio pulled a contrite look over his face. He knew how to fake his feelings. "I am sorry, Papa. It is my friends in this town who are stupid, not you."

His father merely grunted his response. He knew his son was probably insincere. "I will sign the papers with Señor Martinez."

"Please, Papa, let me return to school for one more year. I will study to be an — "

"Ha! You return to school? Impossible. You hated the priest and the good nuns who tried to teach you." Now his father sneered at Antonio's request. "I doubt if Padre Julius would let you return. You were always leading the other students into trouble."

"I beg you, Papa." Antonio dropped to his knees in a dramatic gesture. His expressive brown eyes filled with real tears. "Let me go to the academy. I want to ride with the army of New Spain."

"New Spain?" his father scoffed. "What guarantee do we have that we will still be 'New Spain?' Why not 'New France,' or 'New Austria?' Both countries are keeping their warships off our coast ready to pounce." He shrugged before turning away from his disappointed son. "Even now the military men are talking about complete independence for our country."

No one knows Santa Anna's exact words to his father, because Santa Anna did not write a diary. But history tells the story of Santa Anna so clearly the reader can imagine how he talked and felt as a boy.

Santa Anna, as he would be called, submitted and was apprenticed to the merchant. He was miserable the entire time. Every time a troop of soldiers came riding through Jalapa, Santa Anna promised himself that one day, when he was older, he would ride with the army of whomever was in control of his country.

In the Army of New Spain

Santa Anna stood in front of the mirror as he slid his gloved hands down his thighs, turning this way and that. His uniform, a farewell gift from his parents, fit perfectly. It is good I stood over that old tailor, he thought. My uniform is the finest in the barracks.

At sixteen years old, Santa Anna stood no taller than the average cadet, around five feet nine inches. He was slender, light skinned in color, a true Creole, born in Mexico, the son of a mother and father who had come from Spain. He had a look of confidence, almost arrogance, about his posture and the way he held his head and shoulders.

To him, the vision he saw in the mirror was not a young man in cadet's uniform, but the uniform of a general. He could see the golden epaulets, a crimson ribbon across his chest with many medals covering his heart. Santa Anna still nurtured his childhood dream of becoming a general — the greatest general in all New Spain.

Before his sixteenth birthday, he had finally persuaded his father to permit him to become a cadet in the Fijo de Vera Cruz infantry regiment. Antonio had complained about his work with the merchant. "The women, Papa. How they go on over the cloth. Each piece has to sniffed, stretched, and even tasted before they will buy. And Señor Martinez, he is a slave driver. He says I must run when I deliver merchandise to the homes. Please, Papa," he begged. "It is not a fit job for a real man, only for a weakling." Probably the merchant, Martinez, was equally glad when his unruly apprentice became the responsibility of the army of New Spain.

Santa Anna soon became the favorite of the officers. He was an able fighter, dependable, very ambitious, and eager to learn all he could about military science. During the next five years, Santa Anna was promoted to Lieutenant of Grenadiers of the Second Battalion under General Joaquín de Arredondo. It was with Arredondo's battalion in 1812 that he went to Bexar (San Antonio) to suppress the Gutiérrez-Magee revolt.

Arredondo's battalion of two thousand of Mexico's finest troops traveled across the Rio Grande to the shores of the Medina River to begin the suppression of the Magee-Gutiérrez revolt. Revolutionist Bernardo Gutiérrez and Augustus Magee, a disgruntled lieutenant from the United States army, had joined forces in a revolt against Spain's treatment of Texas, Mexico, and Louisiana.

Gutiérrez and Magee set forth in August, 1812, from Natchitoches with eight hundred soldiers: Anglo-Americans, Mexicans, Texians, Louisiana Frenchmen, mercenaries, and adventurers. They called themselves The Republican Army of the North. They hoped to be victorious in making Texas an official state of Mexico, or become one of the United States of America, or perhaps become a republic — a separate country.

The Republicans met little or no resistance from the Spanish garrison at Nacogdoches. As they moved down across Texas, others joined the ranks. At La Bahia presidio, the army also withstood the Spanish Royalist troops.

This victory and the addition of more volunteer troops sent the Republican Army over to Bexar (San Antonio). Again the army was successful in routing the Royalist Army and the local government.

Victory there was short lived as in the case when men forget their common cause and begin to struggle over power and individual wants. General Arredondo and his troops, including Santa Anna, victorious at the Medina, mercilessly swept through Bexar and as far north as Nacogdoches. Less than one hundred of the alleged two thousand Republican troops survived.

Santa Anna was eighteen years old when he helped murder part of the surrendered Bexar garrison as an object lesson to the men seeking independence from New Spain.

During these five years under General Arredondo, Santa Anna began gambling. Sometimes he won, but much of the time he lost. He finally needed money so badly he forged the names of his commanding officers to some money drafts.

"Lieutenant! You are not only a fool, but an idiot!" shouted Doctor Jaime Garza, the surgeon of Santa Anna's regiment. "How dare you forge Colonel Quintero's signature on drafts on your company's funds?"

Santa Anna did not answer. He knew if he acted sorry or ashamed, the doctor, his friend, would forgive him. Knowing when to fake being sorry for his actions had saved him from many a whipping by his father. He knew the surgeon would loan him the money he needed for his gambling debts. He only had to look sorrowful.

But Doctor Garza had known him for five years. He knew Santa Anna was full of tricks. Even though the doctor planned to get Santa Anna out of trouble by loaning him the money, he was not through lecturing him. Doctor Garza banged his fist against the desktop in his anger. "Why did you do it? If General Arredondo knew you had also forged his signature, you would be shot!"

"I had hoped to — "

"Yes! Hoped to return the money. That is what all

thieves say when caught." The surgeon came from behind his desk and placed himself within a foot of Santa Anna's face. "Take me to your quarters."

Santa Anna, wondering why the doctor wanted to go to his quarters, led the way. He was grateful the man had not refused to loan him the money.

When they arrived in Santa Anna's quarters, Doctor Garza ordered, "Open your chest and place all your possessions on the blanket on your cot."

Santa Anna frowned and made no move to obey.

"Now! You are wasting my time."

Santa Anna pulled his extra clothing, his books, his extra bedding from the chest. He flung each object to the bed. "Why are you making me do this?" he asked, his face almost black with anger.

"The sword, too," demanded the doctor. "I am holding these until you repay me." He looked straight into Santa Anna's eyes. "I do not believe you will repay me."

Sweat gathered on Santa Anna's brow. This time he did not have to fake being sorrowful. "This sword is special to me. It has sentimental value — "

Doctor Garza shrugged. "It has monetary value to me."

"What can I do without my sword?"

"You can say that you lost it and get another from the commissary."

"Those swords from the commissary are so ordinary," Santa Anna complained. His fists clenched to keep from hitting the doctor. "I've worked long and hard for this magnificent Toledo steel bladed sword, and you know that!"

"Do not whine, Lieutenant. Did you think I swallowed that story you made up about taking the money to defend another officer and the honor of the regiment?"

Santa Anna looked down at his empty chest. He could not answer.

The doctor sighed. "You are the fool in this room."

There was nothing Santa Anna could say. He had to have the money to replace what he had taken from his regiment's funds. His hands caressed the hilt of the beautiful sword, then placed it, too, on the cot. After tying the four corners of the blanket together, he followed the doctor back to his clinic. He carried the sword in one hand and his possessions in the other hand. He gritted his teeth as he promised himself he would get the sword back, one way or the other.

At the clinic, Doctor Garza took the sword and the bundle. He counted out the necessary gold that would keep Santa Anna from being expelled from the army of New Spain, or worse still, being shot.

Santa Anna did not stop gambling. Perhaps he became more lucky. It is sad that a man with his personality was lacking in integrity and honor. Later, when Santa Anna was older and running for president of his country, his enemies would remind the voters of Santa Anna's compulsive gambling.

"This young man will live to make his country weep," said the viceroy of New Spain, General O'Donoju.

On November 20, 1815, Santa Anna joined his company in Vera Cruz as military commander of the area outside the city. He, with five hundred men assigned to him, was successful in curbing the mounting revolt of the people. Soon he was wearing the coveted golden epaulets on his shoulders. It was after this that the commanding general awarded him the sought after *Cross of the Royal and Distinguished American Order of Isabella the Catholic.* He began to earn other medals, too.

Seven years later Santa Anna and other generals aroused the people to create a republic, to declare the country free of Spain.

In helping rid Mexico of Spain's control, Santa Anna soon became a wealthy man. His wealth did not come from his small government salary. Generals were expected to take from the land what they wanted: land, money or other resources. Santa Anna took over the estates of his enemies, taxed whomever he wanted.

The time came when Santa Anna decided to marry. Even though he enjoyed being very popular with the ladies, he decided he must marry and produce sons and daughters. Rich, beautiful ladies were eager to become his wife, but Santa Anna did not want a wife who would outshine him at social functions. He was looking for a healthy, submissive young woman who would remain in the background and bear him sons. She must be a young woman who would make no trouble when he was unfaithful to her, for he did not intend limiting himself to the role of a faithful husband.

At one of the elaborate social functions, Santa Anna met the Garcia family. Señor Garcia had two unmarried daughters. Santa Anna had seen them with the family. One was young, beautiful and shy, exactly what he wanted.

As was the custom in those days, Santa Anna did not court the heavily chaperoned girl he had chosen to marry. He was not allowed to tell her of his intentions until he had spoken to her father. Match-making was a cold, legal affair.

Santa Anna met with the girl's father and announced his intentions. They spent the evening discussing this proposed marriage at length until they both could agree on the marriage settlement. Santa Anna finally agreed as to what he would accept as a dowry (money and property) from his bride. The necessary papers were signed before witnesses.

During this transaction there must have been much drinking, for the usually articulate Santa Anna named the wrong Garcia girl. Since there was no courtship, Santa Anna met his bride-to-be for the first time at the altar.

It has been noted that when he saw he had named the less pretty Garcia daughter, he merely shrugged and said, "It is all the same to me."

After the wedding trip, Santa Anna moved his bride into Manga de Clava, his estate located near Jalapa on the road to Vera Cruz. Inez Garcia became the submissive, non-interfering wife Santa Anna wanted. She bore him four sons and a daughter.

CHAPTER THREE

The War Years

Santa Anna's boast to his father, "I will fight with whomever is in charge of our country," soon came true. He was always willing to change loyalties. Even after the generals declared Mexico independent of Spain, in 1822, Mexico was still a country divided. Arguing generals and their patrons, the rich landowners, continued to battle and plunder each others' lands. Santa Anna allied himself with any winning faction.

Most of the generals fought without government pay. It was expected that they could take property, possessions or whatever they could from their foes. Many became quite wealthy.

As a result of winning many battles, Santa Anna often referred to himself as "the Napoleon of the West." His fame grew and, in April of 1833, he was elected president of Mexico for the first time. When not in Mexico City or on the battlefields, Santa Anna was at his beloved estate, Manga de Clava.

To the observer, Manga de Clava's elaborate cock pens seemed more important to Santa Anna than his wife and children. His love for cock fighting and the gambling connected with it was second only to his love for making war. At Manga de Clava, colorful fighting roosters were trained to destroy game cocks from all over Mexico. The cocks, equipped with long, sharp, silver spurs, won only after they had ripped their opponents to death.

Even though he prided himself on being successfully diplomatic in settling disputes, he never evidenced a liking for political bureaucracy. Many times when Santa Anna tired of being president, or sensed he was losing his popularity with the people, he would fake ill health in order to take a leave of absence or to resign the presidency. He would then return to his beloved fighting roosters at Mango de Clava.

The Texas Campaign Begins

After the Gutiérrez-Magee uprising in 1812, Texians, as they were then called, once more submitted as a province to the rule of Mexico. Santa Anna made many promises to the citizens of this part of Mexico. He did not keep those promises. When Santa Anna was elected president for the second time, the Texians thought he would truly represent them. But all the while, there were many Texians wanting to become independent of Mexico.

The unfaithfulness of the government of Mexico and Santa Anna finally forced the revolution of the Texians in 1835. Santa Anna was in retirement at this time at Manga de Clava. He had become so unpopular with the Mexicans he had resigned due to "ill-health," turning the government over to General Barriagan, the vice-president.

News of the insurrection in Texas reached Mexico City, General Barriagan and the cabinet officials. General Santa Anna, upon learning this, fully recovered from his so-called "ill health." He became once more the General of the Army, leaving the country in the hands of the vice-president. All his efforts were put to organizing his army of invasion. By January, 1836, Santa Anna with trained troops and supplies began the march to the Rio Grande.

February, 1836, found El Presidente, as he loved to be called, and his troops camped near the small, fortified mission called the Alamo in Bexar de San Antonio. When, on February 23, the flag of the rebellion still flew over the Alamo, Santa Anna realized the Texians were not frightened by the appearance of several thousand Mexican troops.

Santa Anna did not raise the flag of his own country from the tower of San Fernando Cathedral, the highest point in Bexar. Instead, the Texians could now see and perhaps truly fear the Mexican forces. For Santa Anna flew from the cathedral tower a blood red banner — the sign that El Presidente would take no prisoners. "Death to all!" was the message of the banner and Santa Anna.

By March 4, the walls of the Alamo had been breached by the Mexican battery now positioned within rifle range of the Texians. The exhausted Texians welcomed, but did not understand the sudden quiet that filled the air the evening of March 5. Santa Anna declared his soldiers

Santa Anna flew from the cathedral tower a blood red banner
— a sign that El Presidente would take no prisoners.

needed sleep and food. As they rested, he with his staff made plans for the final assault.

That night, while most of the surviving Texians slept, the Mexican troops, urged on by the notes from the cornet's murderous *deguello* (no quarter given) filling the air, invaded the Alamo. Disappointed that so few Texians remained to be slaughtered, the Mexicans acted as wild men, even mutilating dead bodies. By nine o'clock, March 6, the siege had ended.

Not until the battle was over did Santa Anna join his troops in their battle. When all of the Texians were presumed dead, the walls breached by hundreds of Mexican soldiers, Santa Anna, his staff, and several Bexar citizens loyal to Mexico, entered the mission.

"Show me Crockett, Bowie and Travis," Santa Anna ordered. This was done. Satisfied they were dead, Santa Anna turned to leave the Alamo. One of the Mexican soldiers found a wounded Texian who had been presumed dead. He took the prisoner to Santa Anna and asked what to do with the Texian.

El Presidente stared at the wounded man for a moment. Furious that the man was still alive, he reminded his staff, "No quarter given!" Santa Anna turned his back and waited. Several shots were fired. The final Texian defender of the Alamo was dead.

An estimated sixteen hundred Mexicans were killed, hundreds of others were wounded. Many of those killed were the best trained soldiers of the Mexican army. Santa

Anna was forced to stay for several weeks in Bexar to re-form his army and establish an effective government. This delay in his march north was one of the deciding factors in his defeat later in the battle at San Jacinto.

While still in San Antonio, word came to Santa Anna that Colonel J. W. Fannin and about four hundred Texians had surrendered to General José Urrea near Goliad. Fannin had surrendered on the condition that he and his men would be prisoners-of-war. Santa Anna, angered that General Urrea had recommended clemency, yelled, "No quarter!" On March 27, 1836, three hundred ninety-eight Texians faced a Mexican firing squad. All but the thirty-four soldiers who escaped were shot to death.

When accused of being bloody and unfeeling about this slaughter, Santa Anna reported: " . . . they surrendered unconditionally, as communication from General Urrea shows . . . that neither officially or confidentially was I notified of such a capitulation."

Later on, Santa Anna reported: "The Commander at Goliad, Lieutenant Colonel José Nicolas de la Portilla, is responsible for the cruel and inhumane manner of carrying out the execution to the nation, to the world, and to God."

True to his character, Santa Anna not only would claim credit for others' victories, he insisted others take the responsibility for his unpopular and cruel actions.

The men at the Alamo and Goliad had not died in vain.

All Texians would respond to their noble sacrifices.

"Remember the Alamo!" and "Remember Goliad!" became the battle cries of the outnumbered, but valiant Texians in future battles.

CHAPTER FIVE

San Jacinto

Before the battle at Goliad, General Urrea had written Santa Anna: "I must inform you what kind of an enemy you have to fight. This horde of marauders, the dregs, and the off-scouring of the American people, came out of their own accord to commit their depredations against us, who have never offended. . . . "

It is true there were criminals and unsavory types who had migrated to Texas. However, the majority of the immigrants were of pioneer stock. They wanted to make a better life for themselves and their families. The generals and Creole aristocracy of Mexico considered most of the population of Texas to be no more than "Texian peóns."

Feeling this way, Santa Anna often misjudged his opponents. Sam Houston was one of them. El Presidente heard that Houston and his men were encamped at San Felipe de Austin on the Brazos River. Santa Anna immediately set out to destroy this small threat to Mexican sovereignty. His spies had also reported that Houston's men were deserting their leader. Some Texians had deserted after hearing of the battle of the Alamo and the slaughter at Goliad. Houston had also given permission to some of the family men among his soldiers to return home and move their families out of the predicted path of Santa Anna's army.

General Houston, learning of Santa Anna's approach, burned the town of San Felipe and abandoned the area. Santa Anna believed the rumor that Houston and his men were fleeing in fear to Louisiana. In his report, Santa Anna wrote: "Houston is in the woods at Groce's, eleven leagues away, with only eight hundred men who have stuck to him, and he intends to retire across the Trinity if we cross the Brazos. He is intimidated by the successive triumphs of our army and terrified by our rapid movements."

When Santa Anna learned that members of the Texas provisional government were escaping to Galveston Island, he said he intended to capture the officials and take them to Mexico City as hostages. Observers knew that being Santa Anna, he would be tempted to shoot them as soon as the troops captured the officials.

On April 19, General Houston and his men headed for Harrisburg. From his spies Houston had learned that Santa Anna had only a portion of his troops with him as he tried to follow the escaping Texas government officials headed for Galveston Island. That day Houston and his men camped near where Buffalo Bayou and the San Jacinto River met.

When the Mexican troops failed in capturing the government officials, Santa Anna turned back his forces on April 20. After discovering Houston and his men camped near the river, the Mexican army took a position about a mile away on higher ground. A spongy marsh separated the two armies. Santa Anna, seeing the small size of the Texian army, took his time in setting up his camp and preparing for battle.

"Look at them, they are nothing but rags and tags and undisciplined filibusters (adventurers)," Santa Anna said as he compared the Texians to his troops and those of General Cós who had joined him. By now, he had almost fifteen hundred men under his command. The rest of his eight thousand soldiers were with Generals Urrea, Filisoa, Sesma and Gaona at other locations.

General Houston had only 783 poorly trained men who were lacking in proper military equipment. But he and his men were armed with their battle cry: "Remember the Alamo! Remember Goliad!"

Santa Anna told his aides, "There is no need to hurry. My men need rest and hot food." He laughed derisively before boasting, "When we want to, we will capture or slaughter the Texians." Nearby, beside the campfire, the cornet player polished his silver horn. Was he thinking all he had to do was sound the dreaded *deguello,* and the battle and slaughter would begin and quickly end?

From their campsite, the Texians watched in amazement when they realized the Mexican soldiers were not preparing for battle. Some of the soldiers were wandering in the wooded areas. Some were gathering in groups around small campfires, partially dressed, enjoying the balmy day. Cavalry riders were exercising their horses or watering their mounts down at the river. They, too, wore no jackets and were unarmed.

Houston and his aides waited until the afternoon of April 21, when most of the Mexican soldiers were enjoying their *siestas* (naps). Their officers were partying. Santa Anna was allegedly entertaining a mulatto woman, Emily Morgan, in his satin tent.

Texas's small army was a half mile away from the Mexican camp before the Mexican soldiers realized what was happening. They were half asleep and unprepared. Most of them were out of uniform. They ran about getting into each other's way, causing much confusion. Officers were unmounted, equally dismayed, and giving orders that no one was hearing.

The Texians swooped down on all this confusion, killing or capturing most of the Mexicans. Some of the Mexican soldiers managed to escape into the woods. One of the Mexican staff writers later reported: "Then I saw his excellency (Santa Anna) running about in the utmost excitement, wringing his hands, unable to give an order."

Santa Anna did manage to escape on his horse. He fled

to Vince's Bayou, four miles away. There, his horse bogged down into the mud. Santa Anna was afoot. His statement claimed: "I alighted from the horse and concealed myself in a thicket of dwarf pine. Night came and I crossed the creek with water up to my waist. I found a house that had been abandoned and some articles of clothing which enabled me to change my apparel. At eleven a.m. the next day, I was crossing a large plain and my pursuers over took me."

The Texian report differed slightly. The next day, April 22, a small detachment of Texians, similar to others who were rounding up the escaping Mexicans, came looking for Generals Cós and Santa Anna. There were only three or four Texians in this group, but Santa Anna did not give them any trouble. Barefooted and in his stolen clothes, it is no wonder the Texians thought he was only an ordinary soldier. Santa Anna was noted for his ornate uniforms with their solid gold or silver crested buttons. One of his captors wanted to shoot him on the spot of his capture.

Others insisted he not be shot, and decided to make him walk ahead of them the four miles back to camp. The men laughed and jeered as their captive struggled barefooted over the dry, grassy stubble and twigs, hopping about as he stumbled on pine cones and stepped on grass burrs. Still, Santa Anna did not complain, for although defeated he still showed the courage of his calling.

Finally, a more sympathetic Texian noted Santa Anna's

feet were skinned and bleeding. The Texian pulled ahead of the group and motioned for Santa Anna to mount behind him on his horse. They rode that way to the camp in spite of the jeers of the other Texians.

Even though Santa Anna held his head low, hoping to avoid recognition, cries of "El Presidente! El Presidente!" filled the air. His soldiers recognized the man they considered half-god.

Lorenzo de Zavala, the newly elected vice president of Texas, was Santa Anna's sworn enemy. Near General Houston's tent stood Zavala's son. Santa Anna recognized him and went to embrace him. "Ah, Señor Zavala! At last, a friend. I am so very fond of your father." This ruse did not work. Young Zavala, who was acting as an interpreter, pushed aside his father's enemy.

The men brought Santa Anna to stand in front of Houston, who, because he had been wounded, was reclining on a pallet under a tree. General Houston waited silently for the captured president of Mexico and general of the army to speak.

Arrogant as always, never one to accept defeat, and always ready to talk himself out of danger, Santa Anna, in a very snobbish way, addressed his captor. "You have captured the Napoleon of the West. Surely that is a great honor for you. Because of that, you can afford to be merciful."

General Houston is said to have replied, "What mercy did you show at Goliad or the Alamo?"

The men brought Santa Anna to stand in front of Houston.

Not for the first time, Santa Anna lied. "I did not know they had surrendered. General Urrea deceived me. I will look into the matter, and if I find that they had surrendered, General Urrea will be brutally punished."

General Houston had to leave for New Orleans for treatment of his wound. Against the wishes of his men who wanted Santa Anna shot, Houston turned Santa Anna over to the provisional government. Santa Anna was sent under heavy guard to Velasco, for he was in constant danger of being killed by the bitter Texians.

At Velasco, two treaties were agreed to by Santa Anna and the Texas officials: The Treaty of Velasco provided Santa Anna would not encourage the Mexicans to continue the war with Texas in their battle for independence. The second treaty with Santa Anna was kept secret. This treaty provided Santa Anna would be returned home via Vera Cruz (by sea). He would then arrange with his cabinet for negotiations between Texas and Mexico. This conference was needed to set the Rio Grande as boundary between Texas and Mexico. Santa Anna promised that he would influence his government into recognizing Texas's independence.

Santa Anna was happy to agree to both treaties. Whether he meant to keep them or not was a matter of speculation by the Texians. They could only hope, for Santa Anna appeared willing to betray his country in exchange for his life.

A few hours before Santa Anna was to sail on the

Invincible for Vera Cruz and home, a vessel came up the Brazos River. On board were soldiers who wanted Santa Anna tried and shot right there. With the help of some of the men of Velasco, a riot almost erupted. The citizens of Velasco had hated having Santa Anna in their town. To save his life, Santa Anna was taken under heavy guard up the Brazos River to the home of Doctor Phelps. There he was kept during the hot summer and autumn following his capture.

When Santa Anna's guards at the Phelps's house learned there was a plan being made for his sympathizers to rescue him, Santa Anna was taken from his comfortable quarters, placed in irons, and chained to a large oak tree in the Phelps's yard.

Santa Anna, depressed by such brutal treatment, tried to poison himself. Doctor Phelps prevented his death. Then, Mrs. Phelps saved him when a band of men came to assassinate him. She threw her arms about him and persuaded the men not to kill him.

By October of 1836, Santa Anna had not been returned to Vera Cruz. At the first meeting of the Texas congress, many leaders wanted Santa Anna executed. General Houston, the newly elected president of Texas, persuaded them not to harm Santa Anna. "President Jackson of the United States wants the president of Mexico freed." He seemed to recognize that the president of the United States was looking far into the future. President Jackson wanted to meet with Santa Anna as soon as possible to discuss purchasing part of the Mexican territory for the United States.

Santa Anna was escorted to Washington, D.C. At the many stops along the route, he was treated as a very important man. People were eager to see the president of Mexico. Not all United States citizens were sympathetic with the Texas cause.

Because Santa Anna kept his promise to Sam Houston, recognition of Texas by the United States was accomplished. In his autobiography, Santa Anna claimed President Jackson told him, "If Mexico will recognize the independence of Texas, we will indemnify your country (pay for your losses) with six million pesos."

Santa Anna said he replied to President Jackson, "To the Mexican Congress solely belongs the right to decide that question."

Many Mexican patriots did not want the war between Mexico and Texas to end. General Terán wrote the government in 1836:

"Whoever consents to and refuses to oppose the loss of Texas is a despicable traitor, worthy of being punished a thousand deaths."

When Santa Anna finally reached Manga de Clava, and in face of the Mexican citizens' anger over his having lost the war with Texas, he resigned as president of

This print of General Santa Anna was first published in the United States in 1837.

Mexico and general of the army. His inactivity and depression lasted until a French squadron in 1838 fired on Vera Cruz.

France had never given up its plan to take over Mexico. Its warships were continually patrolling off the coast of Vera Cruz, waiting for an opportunity to take advantage of the unstable Mexican government.

The French warships entered the port when a French citizen, a baker, laid claims against the Mexican government. Soldiers from each side began skirmishing in what was called "The Pastry War."

Santa Anna begged to be used by the Mexican army. He was assigned to Commandant Manuel Rincon at Vera Cruz.

CHAPTER SIX

Santa Anna's Great Sacrifice

Grateful that he was at last being allowed to serve in the army, Santa Anna forced a look of humility to his face. It would not do to offend Commandant Rincon, even though Santa Anna knew himself to be a far better leader. "You will inspect the fortress of Ulua," the Commandant ordered.

Under the protection of darkness, Santa Anna entered the old fortress. There he discovered the fortress, under the command of General Gaona, showed signs of neglect, a lack of armaments, and proper personnel. General Gaona wanted to surrender the fortress. Santa Anna reported the conditions of the fort to Commandant Rincon.

"You must order more armaments, personnel and provisions," Santa Anna said to Rincon.

Commandant Rincon stared at the former general of the army and threw his written report to the floor. With a sneer in his voice he said, "The fortress will be surrendered with Vera Cruz to the French."

Santa Anna, in his sly, unloyal way, complained to the Council at Mexico City. "There was no need to surrender the fortress or Vera Cruz." After Santa Anna had aroused enough public opinion, General Gaona was court-martialed. The people of Mexico City began to clamor for the return of General Santa Anna. Less than a year before they had been expressing their hatred for him in his failure to stop Texas's bid for independence. Now, they called for the "Napoleon of the West" to rid them of the French. Such was Santa Anna's charm and powers of persuasion. Such was the fickleness of the Mexican people — loyal only if Santa Anna could give them victory.

It is said that President Bustamante, a long-time rival of Santa Anna, finally agreed and delegated him to recapture Vera Cruz. It is assumed that Bustamante hoped Santa Anna would be killed in battle.

When Santa Anna arrived, the French warships were pulling out, their mission accomplished. The "Pastry War" had been settled to the satisfaction of the tradesman, the French, and the city of Vera Cruz. Santa Anna, as was his habit in former years, rushed into the city to claim he had chased the French from Vera Cruz.

All would have been well, he would have had another

unearned victory to his credit, except a skirmish broke out between the departing French and a Mexican guardsman.

Santa Anna had ordered the remaining French diplomats to leave Vera Cruz. Thinking they would, he went to sleep in the barracks. The Frenchmen decided against leaving. Santa Anna, awakened by the attack on the barracks where he slept, is said to have run from his room naked, clutching his clothes about him. The French soldiers, who did not recognize him, were said to have let the frightened "unidentified man" pass, merely asking him, "Where is Santa Anna?"

Santa Anna pointed to the room where General Arista slept. He despised and was very jealous of General Arista.

During the skirmish, a Frenchman's rifle shot shattered Santa Anna's lower left leg. He was moved to Pozitos. There, the doctors decided to amputate his leg below the knee.

Thus began the most dramatic time in Santa Anna's life. "Because of me," Santa Anna reported, "the French have left Vera Cruz." Santa Anna thus claimed credit for saving the city. In doing so, he had suffered a hero's wound. The amputation was poorly done, and he would suffer with his leg the rest of his life. Santa Anna gloried in announcing to Mexico and all the world what a great sacrifice he had made. During the rest of his years he would make certain no one forgot his magnificent sacrifice.

At first, after being wounded, he thought he was dying. He did not want the citizens of Mexico to forget him. Even before he had had the necessary medical attention, he penned a seventeen page "death" message to these people in which he wrote:

"*We conquered, yes we conquered:* Mexican arms secured a glorious victory in the plaza; and the flag of Mexico remained triumphant: I was wounded in this last effort and probably this will be the last victory that I shall offer my native land. . . .

"May all Mexicans, forgetting my political mistakes, not deny me the only title which I wish to leave my children: that of a 'good Mexican.' "

He insisted his amputated leg be carried by his soldiers through villages to the cheers and homage of the people. It was finally buried in Pozitos. Later it would be exhumed and buried in an especially built monument in Mexico City when Santa Anna was present and happy to participate in the ceremonies.

From Pozitos he returned to Manga de Clava to recover from his wound. Among his many visitors during this time of convalescence was Madam Calderon, the wife of an Austrian diplomat. In her account of her visit, in 1839, she wrote:

"We arrived about five, at Manga de Clava after passing through leagues of gardens, all the property of Santa Anna. We were received by an aide, and by several officers, and conducted to a large, agreeable apartment, with little furniture. . . . In a little while entered General Santa Anna, a gentlemanly good looking person, with one leg, apparently somewhat an invalid. He was of sallow complexion, fine dark eyes, soft and penetrating, and with an interesting face. Knowing nothing of his past history, one would have said a philosopher, living in dignified retirement — one who had tried the world, and found that all was vanity: one who had suffered ingratitude. It is strange how frequently this expression of philosophic resignation, of placid sadness, is seen in the countenances of the deepest, most ambitious, and most designing men. . . . Altogether he was a polished hero, with quiet and gentlemanly manners. He will not remain here in quiet, for he has within him, according to de Zavala, 'a principle of action, forever impelling him forward.' "

March of 1839 found Santa Anna still enjoying his fame. At the same time, the people were complaining about President Bustamante. Revolution was brewing in some of the states. The public clamored for Santa Anna to return and restore order and unity to the nation. Was it because his flamboyant and dictatorial ways offered stability plus excitement?

Urged by the nation's officials, President Bustamante retired to Tampico. Santa Anna was appointed temporary president. With much ceremony, he was carried on a litter from Manga de Clava to Mexico City.

Santa Anna, not one to sit still when there was a battle

to be fought, learned Generals Urrea and Mejía were leading a revolution in Puebla. Although Santa Anna's followers begged him not to go, he was carried on a litter ahead of his troops.

An advance troop led by General Valencia captured General Mejía and ended the small revolution. Santa Anna, even though he and his troops arrived two days later, and as was his habit, assumed credit for squelching the attempted revolution.

From his litter, Santa Anna disposed of General Mejía, his former friend and comrade. "Let Mejía be shot in an hour."

"He is kind," said the prisoner, General Mejía, when told of his fate. "If I had taken him, I would have shot him in five minutes."

Santa Anna's order to all his generals was: "The firing squad for all captured officers."

Santa Anna, on his litter, was then escorted by his troops back to Manga de Clava. Each village they passed through paid him homage. No one spoke of General Valencia, the true hero. No one mentioned the loss of Texas. They were constantly reminded of his great sacrifice — the loss of his leg. When they arrived at Manga de Clava, Santa Anna wisely returned the office of president to Bustamente. Santa Anna seemed to know it wasn't the time for him to be president.

The people soon turned against Bustamante and forced him to abdicate. The Mexican generals met and appointed

Santa Anna again as interim president. He was able to institute reforms which included building the new market place in the capital, a new customs building, an addition to the wharf at Vera Cruz, and the Santa Anna Theatre.

Yet, these and other improvements in Mexico made little showing against the financially disastrous behavior of Santa Anna.

President Lamar of Texas, in 1841, sent a delegation of businessmen and soldiers to Santa Fe, in the northern Mexican territory. Lamar, ambitious and politically motivated, wanted this vast area of land that stretched to the Pacific Ocean to become a part of the Republic of Texas.

His plan was a pitiful failure. When the weary and inexperienced party arrived at Santa Fe, they discovered Santa Fe citizens did not want to be annexed. The Mexicans and Indians produced such a show of force, the Texans were captured without a shot being fired. The captive Texans were marched to Mexico City where they were placed in the old Spanish castle at Perote.

They were soon joined by other Texans taken in a battle at Mier, a Mexican village south of the Rio Grande. These men were the survivors of two hundred or more Texans who, tiring of the many Mexican raids into Texas, had crossed the border into Mexico. It was their intent to punish the raiders and put a stop to their stealing and killing in Texas.

Unfortunately for the Texans, they did not succeed. At Mier, after their defeat, each Texan had to draw a bean from a clay pot. The 159 men who drew white beans were marched to Perote. The seventeen men drawing black beans were immediately shot.

Upon their arrival in Mexico City, Santa Anna discovered one of the prisoners was Orlando Phelps, the son of Doctor and Mrs. Phelps. He remembered how the Phelps had saved his life twice after the battle at San Jacinto. Santa Anna immediately released Orlando Phelps and provided him with transport back to Texas. This is one of the *good* deeds recorded in Santa Anna's favor.

President Sam Houston and the Texas Congress, in 1844, finally secured the release of those Texans who had survived the horrible conditions of the dungeons of Perote.

CHAPTER SEVEN

The Ambush

From 1841 to 1843, Santa Anna was the complete despot. His liberal ideas were forgotten. He became an absolute ruler, almost a dictator. He used his country's tax money for his own benefit. He bought estates, town property, and threw lavish parties for his friends.

Everything he owned had to be the best. His residences were decorated with the finest furniture, satin drapes, and Persian carpets. Gardeners tending his many estates were paid with government tax money. He even encouraged his lesser officials to follow his example. They were allowed to dip into the treasury, too. This shameless, extravagant behavior finally enraged the poor, tax-paying people. The patriotic and influential men of Mexico also began to protest. Santa Anna knew that it was once more time to plead ill-health. In 1843, he resigned and returned to his pens of game cocks and the gambling sessions at Manga de Clava.

Antonio Lopez de Santa Anna

The observing world was indeed surprised when the Mexican people again, in 1844, re-elected Santa Anna as president. Although he was elected in January, he did not take office until June of that year. A magnificent inaugural celebration was held in Mexico City. A bronze statue of Santa Anna was unveiled. Santa Anna stood resplendent in a new, more ornate uniform as the dedicatory address was given. It was fiesta time for the privileged.

Santa Anna did not profit from his former mistakes. He resumed his lavish lifestyle. He entertained important dignitaries from all over the world. The government of the separate states of Mexico suffered.

In Puebla, Doña Inez Garcia, Santa Anna's wife and the mother of his five children, lay dying. Her death came on August 23, 1844. In his memoirs, Santa Anna wrote, "Greater sorrow I had never known!" Still, three months later, at the age of fifty, he married fifteen-year-old Maria Doloras Tosta.

Finally, sensing the growing opposition of the people, Santa Anna offered his resignation. But when friends insisted he return to the capital, he withdrew his resignation. His opposition grew.

The people of Mexico kept urging him to go back and retake Texas. He paid no attention to the people or made many promises with no intention of keeping them. He had emptied his country's treasury with his many extravagances. Now, the same Santa Anna who had always loved making war, did not seem to care about regaining Texas. Soon he was back at Manga de Clava enjoying his so-called ill-health and his game cocks.

In his greedy, self-serving way, Santa Anna did not seem to realize he was doing Texas a favor. Tax money that should have been going into the Mexican treasury to build and equip an army was passing through Santa Anna's pockets to support his lifestyle.

An excerpt of one of the many anti-Santa Anna printed notices at that time read:

"Genius of evil, and covetousness! You are like Attila the scourge of God! Your power had been like that of Satan, a power of corruption, of ruin and destruction! You resemble a fury of hell, blind, devastating and bloody! Amid the horrors of civil war, amid lakes of blood and mountains of dead bodies you always present yourself like a spectre, inciting all to devastation, slaughter, and revenge . . . "

The citizens of Guadalajara with General Paredes and his troops finally revolted against Santa Anna's government. The interim president in Mexico City ordered Santa Anna to take his troops from Jalapa and proceed to Guadalajara and put down the revolution.

While on the way to Guadalajara he received word that another revolt had started in Mexico City. The interim president had been imprisoned by the revolutionaries. To Santa Anna's added horror, the message also said rioters

This political cartoon shows Santa Anna with his game cocks on his back.

in Mexico City, the ones who had been quick to shout Santa Anna's praises, had broken into the elaborate burial tomb of his leg. Tying a string around the gruesome remains of his leg, they had drug it down the street of the city, mocking him and his "great" sacrifice for Mexico.

Upon the heels of this messenger came another one. He brought word that the government had ordered a court of impeachment for Santa Anna. He knew it was time to resign. Santa Anna dispatched a messenger to Mexico City asking the revolutionary government to accept his resignation, and to make plans for him and his family to enter exile. When the government refused both requests, Santa Anna tried to escape to Jalapa. From there he planned to take his family to Vera Cruz. There they would board a ship to exile and safety.

Separated from his troops, Santa Anna and three companions thrust through the woods on seldom used trails on the side of the mountain near Jalapa. He disguised himself as a mule skinner and, against the wishes of his alarmed companions, Santa Anna pushed on even though spotted by a stranger who fled into the woods ahead of them.

Suddenly shots rang out. The mules panicked. Santa Anna's companions jumped from the wagon and disappeared, leaving Santa Anna to face the attackers. Hindered by his wooden leg, he could not jump or run. His attackers pulled him from the wagon to the ground.

They were not bandits, but Indians of the area.

The Indians of Mexico feared and hated Santa Anna. These were from a nearby village and probably some of the Indians Santa Anna had forced to serve in his army. Whenever he needed to raise an army, his press gangs or soldiers would herd Indians into the front lines. Santa Anna gave them little training or equipment. They were to be only cannon fodder. Santa Anna intended them to be a human barricade between the enemy and his trained soldiers.

The Indians took him into their village, Xico. At first they did not recognize him but, when they stripped his clothes off, they discovered his wooden leg. Word had come that the army was searching for him. "El Gordo!" (the fat one) they shouted. They would take him to Mexico City — perhaps for a reward. But first, they would give him a taste of their own revenge. There they forced him to go through a weird, crude and torturous ceremony. Here among the Indians, his eloquence and charisma could not save him. The Indians ripped off his uniform. They jeered at his wooden leg. They took it and tried to use it, lashing it to their bent knees. He suffered other indignities at the hands of the squaws.

The Indians' plan was to cover his naked body in oil and spices. Then they would wrap him in banana leaves, tying them in place with strips of bear grass. The water in the large clay vat was set to boil.

They planned to boil him in the water until he was

dead, but take him out while his flesh was still firm. The women were busy making a vast amount of masa paste. This would be placed around his body, making him into a giant tamale. Once the tamale cooled, they would haul him by cart to Mexico City and there deliver him to the new government.

Years later, a woman from Xico would relate this story that her grandmother, a witness, had told her. A local Catholic priest, fearing the mounting enthusiasm of the Indians, rang the church bell fast and furiously. It was ironic that Santa Anna, after having criticized the leaders of the Catholic Church in Mexico for so many years, was rescued from humiliation and certain death by one of its priests. The harsh clanging of the bell seemed to quiet the hecklers. They turned to see the priest carrying his holy vessel containing the Host walk into their midst. He demanded that the Indians release Santa Anna and turn him over to the government troops. They obeyed. Soon he was in the hands of the authorities at Jalapa.

He did not make a model prisoner. His arrogance and demands soon became too much for the local prison. He was sent to the dungeons of the fortress of Perote. This fortress sat on a cliff that towered a thousand feet above the sea. He was placed in the same dungeons he had inhumanely cast the Texas survivors of the ill-fated Santa Fe and Mier expeditions. Many of their graves lay outside the walls of the fortress.

The Ambush

On December 5, 1844, because he was afraid for his life, Santa Anna abdicated from the presidency of Mexico. This particular date meant nothing to the Mexican citizens except that they were once again rid of Santa Anna. To him, the date brought desolation. Had his countrymen forgotten so soon? Didn't they remember his terrible sacrifice? December 5 was the sixth anniversary of Pozitos, the day he lost his leg fighting the French.

The government finally granted him exile for life. In June, 1845, Santa Anna and his young wife sailed for Havana, Cuba, on their way to a life as exiles in Venezuela.

CHAPTER EIGHT

Havana

Santa Anna, his wife and servants were to stay only a few days in Havana while they waited passage to Venezuela. To their surprise and delight, Captain General Leopolo O'Donnell of Havana learned of their presence on the ship. His aide came with O'Donnell's own boat to take them ashore to be his guests.

Santa Anna was entertained and appreciated by the people in Havana. Because of this, he decided to spend his exile in Cuba.

Even though he had been disgracefully discarded by his own country, Santa Anna maintained an avid interest in the happenings in Mexico. He learned of the beginning of the United States and Mexico's dispute over what boundary line should separate the two countries. Santa Anna, wanting to return to Mexico in any way he could, sent an emissary to the president of the United States. In his message to President Polk, Santa Anna claimed that he, and only he could resolve the boundary dispute. President Polk believed what the wily Santa Anna claimed. He allowed Santa Anna's ship to slip through the U. S. Navy's blockade of Mexican ports.

Santa Anna had no intention of influencing the Mexican government to settle with the United States. He was only interested in being restored as the leader of his country. This was only another promise Santa Anna would break.

When Texas became a state, in 1846, Mexico claimed the Nueces River near Corpus Christi should be the boundary line between Texas and Mexico. The United States called the Rio Grande the boundary. At this same time, President Polk of the United States was trying to buy the lands called the New Mexico territory and Alta California. These lands included what are presently the states of New Mexico, Arizona, Utah, Nevada, the western part of Colorado, and all of California. For these lands, the United States was offering Mexico thirty million dollars.

Mexico refused the offer and on April 23, 1846, declared war on the intruders, for already American pioneers and their prairie wagons were rolling across and occupying the lands west of the Mississippi. In California, sporadic skirmishes between the newcomers and the Spanish/ Mexican landowners were taking place. The immigrants wanted to make California part of the United States.

General Zachary Taylor, sent earlier by President Polk to protect American interests and citizens, moved his headquarters from the Nueces River near Corpus Christi to the banks of the Rio Grande. There he camped and built what would be called Fort Brown. Later, the city of Brownsville would be born in this location. Several engagements with the Mexican Army resulted in the Mexicans fleeing back across the river. On May 13, 1846, President Polk declared war on Mexico.

CHAPTER NINE

Home Again

Disenchanted with the present government and the way the war was going, Mexican citizens began to clamor for the return of Santa Anna, and the city of Vera Cruz mutinied against the government. On August 16, Santa Anna entered Vera Cruz, where he received all the pomp and ceremony he craved. On September 15, he entered Mexico City.

Since Santa Anna had depleted the country's treasury with all his excesses, there was no money to equip an army. He tried to coerce the wealthy Catholic Church into financing the needed army. The leaders of the Church had longer memories than the citizens of Mexico. Santa Anna had stood against the Church for many years. They refused financial aid.

With his usual arrogance, Santa Anna did not accept their refusal as final. He conceived an elaborate plan to shame the Church into doing what he wanted them to do — lend Mexico the millions of pesos he needed to equip his army. He staged a magnificent show of making a pilgrimage to the Shrine of the Virgin of Guadalupe. There, in front of the people and, of course, many newspaper reporters, he begged the patron saint of Mexico to invoke divine aid, to help his country find the needed money to equip a suitable army. "We must defend our land," he pleaded. He made certain the reporters viewed this act of humility. The papers reporting this plea quoted him as saying, "Since the present war was for the preservation of our adorable religion, the clergy should add to their prayers a contribution of church wealth, in aid of the cause."

The clergy were not impressed. They recognized Santa Anna for the man he was, a sly, underhanded, self-seeking despot who truly had no love for the Church.

For once, Santa Anna had much difficulty in raising money and troops for his army. Certainly he must have used what men he had to go out and round up Indians for his usual cannon fodder. He was even willing to use some of his own money, for he had great wealth, to procure equipment. Many in the government complained that Santa Anna still had expensive tastes. He was spending more on elaborate uniforms and other nonessentials than properly equipping his army.

Still, in three months time he had raised and trained an army of twenty thousand men. How poorly trained the men were would become evident on the battlefields. Surprisingly, he hesitated to take the men out to engage the American forces. The leaders of the nation pleaded with him to fight. The newspapers criticized his reluctance. Santa Anna, although in command, was wary of his Mexican enemies. It was as though he was constantly looking over his shoulder, fearing he would be betrayed by one of his own. Since he was a master at doing just that, Santa Anna lived in fear another leader would gain popularity with the fickle citizens. Santa Anna did not want to be sent into exile again.

The American armies swept across the Rio Grande, defeating the northern generals, taking Matamoros and Monterrey as well as intimidating the people who lived in the countryside.

General Taylor's troops won many skirmishes with the Mexican forces. However, the American army's greatest enemy was sickness. Dysentery, yellow fever, insect bites and exhaustion riddled the ranks of General Taylor's command. Learning this, President Polk became alarmed at the slow progress of the war. Although he did not like General Winfield Scott, Commander of the U.S. Army, President Polk sent him to Mexico to take charge of the war there.

In February, 1847, General Taylor's depleted forces were at Buena Vista, a mountain pass town. Santa Anna and his poorly trained forces marched three hundred miles north to engage the American forces there. By the time of their arrival, Santa Anna's soldiers were practically scarecrows. The money for food had disappeared. They were ragged, hungry, exhausted and inexperienced. Many had deserted by this time. History tells that the men were on half-rations. One historian wrote that the only food available when they made camp was Santa Anna's eight crates of his fighting game cocks.

It was estimated that Santa Anna had lost five thousand troops along the way, leaving him with fifteen thousand soldiers to General Taylor's forty-five hundred.

On February 22, Santa Anna and his troops prepared to meet the American forces. Wrongly thinking that Taylor was in retreat, and in spite of his own unpreparedness, Santa Anna, with his usual arrogance and belief in himself, sent a messenger under a white flag with this communique to General Taylor.

"You are surrounded by twenty thousand men, and cannot in any human possibility avoid suffering a rout, and being cut to pieces with your troops. But as you deserve consideration and particular esteem, I wish to save you from a catastrophe, and for that purpose give you this notice, in order that you might surrender at discretion, under the assurance that you will be treated with the consideration belonging to the Mexican character, to which end you be granted an hour's time to make up your mind, to commence from the moment when my flag of truce arrives at your camp. With this view, I assure you of my particular consideration."

General Taylor replied, "I beg leave to say that I decline acceding to your request."

FLIGHT OF SANTA ANNA FROM THE BATTLE OF CERRO GORDO

After the February battle at Buena Vista with the forces of General Taylor, the American forces of General Scott, advancing from Vera Cruz, were victorious at the battle of Cerro Gordo on April 18, 1847. This picture shows Santa Anna without his wooden leg.

Did Santa Anna immediately order the cornet player to sound the dreaded *deguello*? No, to plan to take prisoners was not his style. Nor did he raise his bloody red flag that signalled *no quarter*. How could he offer to show consideration when he had never shown consideration before to his enemies? Who would believe him? Santa Anna had offered a bluff, and it had been called by General Taylor.

Thus began Santa Anna's greatest battle. Fifteen hundred more American soldiers arrived to help Taylor and his men. That night, the exhausted Americans slept on the cold wet ground without the heat of campfires. The next morning the United States Army rallied to fight only to discover it had no opponent! During the night Santa Anna and his troops had retreated, taking a captured American cannon. Santa Anna claimed victory at Buena Vista as did General Taylor. Perhaps this is the place where the expression "A Mexican stand-off!" was first penned.

The war in the northern states of Mexico was over as far as the Mexican generals were concerned. Santa Anna pushed his troops southward to prepare for the coming of General Winfield Scott and his troops. The Americans had arrived and had been victorious in Vera Cruz. General Scott and his men were now en route to Mexico City.

CHAPTER TEN

Chapultepec

"Here come the Yankees," cried the Mexican soldiers as they streamed into Mexico City with their wounded and dead. The Americans had completely demoralized the Mexican soldiers as a result of the battles at Contreras and Churubusco.

Historians quote José Fernando Ramírez who wrote, "Everything, everything has been lost except our honor. That was lost a long time ago."

The Americans thought that the Mexicans were ready to meet and talk peace. General Scott dispatched a letter that read in part, "Too much blood has already been shed in this unnatural war between the two great Republics of this Continent."

Thinking that General Scott had asked for the armistice, Santa Anna sent a prompt reply. On August 24, both sides agreed on a truce that would last forty-eight hours. Instead, the truce lasted two weeks. General

Scott's men objected to the truce. They wanted to occupy Chapultepec Castle immediately and get on with the war. Mexico City was so very close. But the truce declared that neither country would improve their positions. General Scott had promised, and did honor the requirements of the truce.

Santa Anna, as usual, failed to keep his promise. He immediately began to strengthen his troops' positions. Santa Anna could not legally talk peace. The Mexican government, so disillusioned by Santa Anna's failure to chase the Yankees out of Mexico, would not allow him to negotiate any settlements with the U. S. Army or their representatives.

During the two weeks, Santa Anna had brought together from the outlying areas a force of eighteen thousand soldiers. This number was over twice the number of General Scott's active soldiers.

The battle resumed September 7 with the Mexicans' increased forces. General Scott's men were not happy at the delay and with their unpreparedness. One said, "And now, alas, we have our fighting to do over again."

Mexico City could only be approached over eight causeways that spanned the marshes surrounding the city. Each gate, or *garita*, to Mexico City was not just a gate, but a wide plaza surrounded by buildings each heavily armed with cannon and riflemen.

The Americans were stopped at Molino del Rey. They were almost victorious at Casa Mata and finally the

Mexicans retreated until Santa Anna appeared on the scene. He was able to rally his forces toward Chapultepec. Many American soldiers were killed.

Chapultepec Castle, once the summer palace of an Aztec prince, stood on a hill above one of the western causeways that led into Mexico City. The ancient castle, since 1833, had served as Mexico's National Academy where young boys and men were trained for the Mexican army. Chapultepec Castle contained the famed Halls of Montezuma, the famous Aztec ruler. The Marine activity here, before and after the battle, made history for the United States Marine Corps.

The "Marine Hymn" begins with these words:

"From the Halls of Montezuma
to the shores of Tripoli . . . "

The castle grounds were beautifully landscaped. There were parade grounds and formal gardens surrounded by a thick retaining wall. The castle and grounds perched on top of the hill that stood two hundred feet above the flat lands surrounding the hill.

This position provided the Mexican army with a clear view in every direction. The Americans bombarded the castle for fourteen hours on September 12. The general in charge of the Mexican forces knew the castle would fall to the Americans because of their cannons' constant bombardment. He sent word to Santa Anna for reinforcements.

But Santa Anna was more concerned about the

southern approaches into Mexico City. He sent word that if necessary, he would send troops. But he never did. Some of General Bravo's men, disheartened, began to desert, leaving him with only half of what he needed to continue the fight at the castle.

About fifty of the cadets of the academy decided to stay and fight. Some of these boys were no older than thirteen. They must have felt that since the academy was training them to be soldiers and officers they should remain and serve their country.

The battle raged, first in the Mexicans' favor, and then in the Americans' favor. Finally it became a battle of saber and sword. Bayonets entered and exited from the bodies of both Americans and Mexicans.

The young cadets vainly fought the invaders. The legend tells that the young cadets who had refused to desert their school fought to the end. One thirteen-year-old confronted an American bayonet charge. "Halt!" he called. An American ran his bayonet through the cadet before he was able to shoot. Another cadet lowered the Mexican flag to keep it out of the hands of the Americans. He took the flag and ran across the roof top toward a stairway. Halted by a bullet, he fell off the roof to the rocks far below, still holding the flag.

Six boys were killed. An American correspondent covering the war said the boys died "fighting like demons." Ever since then, every Mexican school child would learn of the *Los Niños Heroicos* — the heroic children.

The battle for Chapultepec was over in an hour after the first charge. The American flag was raised over the castle. A Mexican officer, watching the end of the battle, and standing near Santa Anna, is said to have muttered, "God is a Yankee."

Santa Anna did not stay to see Mexico City surrender to the Americans. Taking what troops he had left, he headed toward Guadalupe Hidalgo. But first he resigned as president of Mexico. From Guadalupe Hidalgo, Santa Anna and his troops marched toward Puebla. On October 9, at Huamantla, he staged a counterattack, led by himself, against the American forces there.

It was the last battle he would fight in the U.S.–Mexican War. The new Mexican government ordered him to give up his commission and to prepare to stand charges about his misconduct of the war. Where were the throngs of citizens who had hailed his return to Mexico?

The following January, he sought permission and received it to leave the country he had served so long, but not necessarily well.

On February 2, 1848, the Mexican government accepted and signed *The Treaty of Guadalupe Hidalgo* in the village of the same name. The treaty set the boundary between the United States and Mexico, from the Gulf of

Mexico to the Pacific Ocean, for there had been fighting in California during this same period. In the treaty, the United States granted Mexico fifteen million dollars cash and assumed three and a quarter million dollars of Mexico's debts. This was a disastrous decision by the Mexican government. They lost about half their country. Later on, the Gadsden Purchase of 1853 would settle an additional boundary dispute between the United States and Mexico.

Santa Anna, meanwhile, prepared for exile again. In April of 1848, he and his family departed for Jamaica. They lived there until April of 1850, at which time they moved to Turbaco, Nueva Granada (Colombia). Santa Anna purchased a small estate he called "La Rosita." He planned to spend the rest of his days there. He even had a crypt prepared for his burial on the land.

CHAPTER ELEVEN

Forgiven
and Recalled

By 1850 Mexico was again torn by politics and revolution. The Mexican congress finally passed a decree that a dictator should be provided for Mexico to ensure unity. It must be someone who lived outside of Mexico. Santa Anna was the only one who fit both qualifications. He and his family once more made the trip back to Mexico and to the thunderous greetings of the citizens who had very short memories. In March of 1853, he was again elected president of Mexico.

The conservative citizens hoped that Santa Anna would be firm in his ruling. They hoped he could, with his charisma, weld the nation together again. They hoped he had learned something from his former mistakes. They hoped in vain.

Santa Anna did institute some reforms. But the good he did was once more overshadowed by his lavish lifestyle. He squandered the peoples' tax money on his home at Jalapa, now practically a palace. Beautiful women and famous men gathered at his home for splendid entertainments. Artists and important singers and literary persons came and stayed for weeks.

As usual, the game cocks and the gambling were the chief attractions. Santa Anna's powerful supporters began to desert him.

When disgruntled citizens revolted in the southern provinces, Santa Anna led his troops down to stop them. Though successful, Santa Anna lost many troops and supplies. It was an expensive victory. Then famine, cholera and drouth struck Mexico. These acts of nature should not have been blamed on Santa Anna, but they were. There were always ambitious politicians ready to smear his name.

Meanwhile, the United States wanted to buy more land from Mexico. In a dispatch from United States Minister John Forsyth to Secretary of State Lewis Cass, Forsyth wrote:

"While all admit that General Santa Anna was the greatest plunderer the Nation has ever owned as a ruler, all unanimously agree, that apart from this, he was the best ruler of the Nation . . . while, as a firm and energetic magistrate, causing his Gov't to be feared and obeyed, no other President has approached him . . . Many Mexicans hold, that the Public treasures he notoriously absorbed, were more than compensated by the energy of his

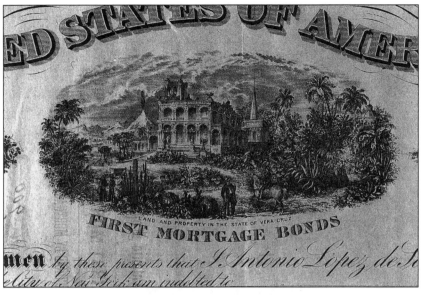

This detail from a mortgage bond (see page 80) shows Santa Anna's palace at Manga de Clavo.

Gral. D.ⁿ Antonio Lopez de Santa Anna, dos veces presidente de la república federal, dos en la central y dictador en 1841 y 1853, con el título de Alteza Serenísima en su última época gubernativa.

Litog. de la V. de Murguia é hijos

administration, the order & safety which existed under it."

Forsyth continued: "I may remark, in passing, that I should have stronger hopes of making a favorable Treaty with Santa Anna, than I have with the present Gov't. Santa Anna *will* have money, & he is not afraid to sell Territory if that be necessary to obtain it."

December 16, 1853, a decree was made giving Santa Anna additional time as dictator. It also said he was to be addressed as "Most Serene Highness."

Mexico needed money so badly that they were ready once more to listen to the United States' offer for some land needed to build a transcontinental railroad. This was only 45,000 square miles of the Mesilla Valley in New Mexico and Arizona. When the threat of a war over the land became obvious, Santa Anna called the people to vote on the Gadsden Purchase. The people agreed to the purchase by the United States for ten million dollars. The treaty of sale was signed on December 30, 1854.

The following months found Mexico again in a state of turmoil and revolution. Santa Anna resigned, naming his successor. August 11, 1855 found Santa Anna and his family once more sailing from Vera Cruz, heading for exile.

CHAPTER TWELVE

One More Time

During the next five years in Turbaco, Nueva Granada, Santa Anna kept in touch with what was happening in Mexico. He was especially excited to learn that France, England and Spain had installed the Archduke of Austria as the "Emperor of Mexico" at the request of some of the people. Here was a new challenge for Santa Anna.

He left for Vera Cruz in the early part of February, 1864. He was questioned about his intentions, but was able to convince the authorities he meant well. He was not believed and ordered by the French to leave the country.

From his estate, he read and learned of what was happening in Mexico. The Emperor Maximilian was having many problems. In order to remind the Mexican citizens he knew of and sympathized with their problems, Santa Anna issued his *Manifesto* of July 8, 1865. It read:

"LIBERALS AND CONSERVATIVES! Let us forget our fraticidal contests and go forward! Let us unite against the common enemy. One single flag covers us, the flag of liberty; one single thought animates us, that of war to the death against the invaders who destroy our towns and kill our brothers. Eternal hatred to the tyrants of our Native Land.

"Fellow citizens! On the memorable 2nd of December, 1822, I took a motto these words: *Down with the Empire! Long live the Republic!* Now from the foreign soil on which I find myself, I repeat it with the same enthusiasm."

Santa Anna was determined to return to Mexico even though he was now sixty-four years old.

Benito Juárez: The Ending

In his eagerness and determination to return to Mexico, Santa Anna traveled to the United States. There he tried to interest influential persons into helping him make his return. At first, various individuals led him on to believe they would help him. But they did not.

Pro-Juárez sentiment of the North Americans defeated his efforts to raise money at every turn. Even the Mexicans living in the United States began to turn against him. Lack of funds forced him to live a much simpler life than he was accustomed to enjoying. The winter of 1866 was a hard one for El Presidente. He had equally poor luck in trying to recruit filibusters or mercenaries to return with him to Mexico.

While living that winter on Staten Island, New York, Santa Anna hired an interpreter named James Adams to

In 1866 while in the United States, Santa Anna attempted to raise money by issuing mortgage bonds on his homes.

act as his secretary. Young Adams was a native of the United States with a natural curiosity about Mexican culture and eating habits. Adams would watch Santa Anna cut a slice from the fruit of the *sapodilla* and chew it, but not swallow it. When Adams questioned his employer about the fruit, he learned this was called *chicle*, a product loved by the Indians and Mexicans.

Adams, astute and very enterprising, asked Santa Anna to give him his supply of *chicle* when Santa Anna left for Mexico in May, 1867. Historians relate that Adams experimented with Santa Anna's *chicle*, mixing various flavors and sweetening agents with it until he had a product he could market. James Adams formed the Adams Chewing Gum Company. It is well that Santa Anna was partially responsible for the developing of chewing gum. But it is sad that this is the only thing El Presidente accomplished in his stay in the United States.

Meanwhile, supporters in Mexico were writing and urging him to come to Mexico to reunite the country. Disillusioned by the lack of support from his so-called connections in the United States, Santa Anna set sail for Vera Cruz.

Emperor Maximilian was having great difficulties in ruling his disorganized country. The generals in some of the provinces were encouraging and leading some of the provinces to protest or revolt against the French rule.

Wanting to believe that he would be welcomed with great fanfare when the ship, the *USS Virginia*, docked at

Vera Cruz, Santa Anna stood anxiously waiting on the deck of the ship. To his dismay he was not allowed to enter the city even though many of his supporters were allowed to visit him there on the ship.

Santa Anna wanted to be back in his native land so much he was willing to swear allegiance to whomever was in power. First, he claimed he had returned to support the Empire. The French were not fooled. Next, he swore he was there to help reestablish the Republic of Mexico. The Mexican authorities were not fooled. They had declared him a traitor in earlier days. They had taken all his wealth and property from him. And, there was Benito Juárez to consider.

Benito Juárez was an Indian, the lowest in the caste system in Mexico, yet he was destined to become one of Mexico's finest statesmen. The rich and privileged called him a radical. In 1853, when Santa Anna was dictator, he had called Juárez a "rabble rousing patriot" and had exiled him from Mexico.

Juárez had returned to Mexico when Santa Anna had in turn been exiled. Juárez brought much needed reform when he was elected president of the Republic.

Santa Anna hated him. Here was one of those despised Indians aspiring to greatness. Even though Santa Anna recognized Juárez's worth, he feared him. Juárez hated Santa Anna and had no respect for the aging despot.

When Emperor Maximilian was assassinated, Juárez took complete control of the country. Santa Anna, still

Benito Juárez

on the *USS Virginia,* was taken off and placed on the U.S. man-of-war *Tacony.* Juárez kept him prisoner there until he was later transferred to the *Virginia* scheduled to leave for Havana.

Rebels boarded the *Virginia* and took Santa Anna to the home of the commandant of Sisal, a port on the Yucatán coast. Still a prisoner, Santa Anna remained there for four days before he was sent to Campeche. There he was kept in prison for two months. If it had not been for relatives and friends, he would have starved to death.

Juárez was determined to bring him to trial as a traitor. The president sent Santa Anna to the dreaded dungeons of Ulua to await his trial. Again Santa Anna was dependent on relatives and friends for food, clothing, and bedding.

When the time for the trial finally arrived, Juárez and his followers demanded the death penalty for the aging general. Fear of reprisal caused Santa Anna's former officers and government officials to refuse to testify in his behalf. Because of the eloquence of Santa Anna's attorney, a special council of the government granted Santa Anna exile instead of death. On November 12, 1867, he and his family were placed on a ship bound for Havana and exile.

When Benito Juárez died in 1872, Santa Anna began his letter writing campaign asking Mexico to let him return. He waited and waited for permission. Finally, the letter came telling him that the Liberal Party of Mexico had granted him amnesty. It did not take him long to make his plans for returning.

Once more he stood at the bow of the ship waiting for expected cheering and a rousing welcome. It did not happen. It was 1874 and he was eighty years old, crippled and half blind. He had outlived most of his peers. There were no crowds as in the past who had praised his every victory. Just a few friends and relatives met the boat at Vera Cruz when it docked. When he finally arrived in Mexico City, the newspapers of the day reported his arrival. One, the *Monitor Republicano*, on March 4, 1874, commented: "In the hour of pardon, and forgetfulness, Mexico does not remember the great political errors of the man who so long controlled its destinies. . . . The Republic today stands with majesty on the throne of peace, and can forget mistakes and open its doors to the one it kept in exile so long."

When the near destitute Santa Anna appealed to the courts for the restitution of his properties, he was denied by the Congress of Liberals. The *Monitor Republicano* declared: ". . . he [Santa Anna] is now an example of human life: a criminal who still walks the earth bearing in his conscience the mark of remorse." The writer of the article continued to explain that the old general was entitled to pity, but nothing else. He was to be considered as one who had been forgiven for having betrayed his country, caused bloodshed, and encouraged civil strife.

The days that followed were not happy ones for Santa Anna. No one seemed to remember or even wanted to hear him tell of his service to Mexico. Almost penniless, he wandered the streets with the help of his wife and kin. El Presidente had returned to his homeland and no one seemed to care.

When a doctor told Santa Anna he could remove the blinding cataracts, Santa Anna is reported to have said, "If being blind, I suffered so many ingratitudes on returning to my home land — what would I see if you again returned my sight? No, I do not wish to see; leave me sunk in darkness, I am more tranquil thus."

Historians report that one man, a lowly peasant, did come to see the aging general. He reminded Santa Anna of the time the people of Mexico City had torn down the monument to Santa Anna's leg, tied a string around it and drug it through the city. "My wife and I found the bones and kept it hidden for years. It was like a sacred relic to us. We finally made a grave for them." Perhaps humility had finally come to Santa Anna. He is said to have kissed the old peasant on the head and thanked him.

Santa Anna died June 21, 1876. Only a few attended his funeral and burial in the village of Guadalupe Hidalgo.

Tomb of Santa Anna and his wife in Guadalupe Hidalgo.

Obituary of
Santa Anna

The last hours of his life inspire the saddest of reflections: the man who controlled millions, who acquired fortune and honors, who exercised an unrestricted dictatorship, who died in the midst of greatest want, abandoned by all except a few of his friends who remembered him in adversity. A relic of another epoch, our generation remembered him for the misfortunes he brought upon the republic, forgetting the really eminent services he rendered to the nation. He was a tree stricken in years, destitute of foliage, to whose boughs even such parasites as are usually found on dry and withered trees did not cling.

— printed in the newspaper *El Siglo Diez y Nueve*

Bibliography

Castañeda, C. E., *The Mexican Side of the Texan Revolution*, Graphic Idea.

Crawford, Ann Fears, ed., *The Eagle: The Autobiography of Santa Anna*, Austin, State House Press, 1988.

Fehrenbach, T. R., *Fire and Blood*, MacMillan.

Haley, James L., *Texas: An Album of History*, New York, Doubleday & Company, 1985.

Haslip, Joan, *The Crown of Mexico*, Holt, Rinehart & Winston, 1971.

Jones, Oakah L. Jr., *Santa Anna*, New York, Twayne Publishers, Inc., 1968.

Meier, Matt S. and Rivera, Feliciano, *Dictionary of Mexican American History*, Westport, Conn., Greenwood Press, 1981.

Myers, John Myers, *The Alamo*, University of Nebraska Press, 1948.

Nevin, David, ed., *The Mexican War*, Time-Life Books, 1978.

Pearson-Procter-Conroy, *Texas: The Land and Its People*, Dallas, Hendrick-Long Publishing Co., 1978.

Simpson, Leslie Byrd, *Many Mexicos*, Berkeley, University of California, 1967.

Strode, Hudson, *Timeless Mexico*, Harcourt, Brace and Company, 1944.

Wharton, Clarence R., *El Presidente: A Sketch of the Life of Santa Anna*, Austin, Gammell Book Store, 1926.

Index

INDEX